MW01205417

The Financial Story Of David Tepper

From Pittsburgh to Wall Street Unraveling the Mind and Success of a Financial Maverick

Henderson J.Smith

In the tapestry of words woven within these pages, a profound symphony of gratitude resonates, echoing the heartfelt appreciation that dances in the spaces between sentences. As a writer, I embark on this journey with a heart brimming with thanks, eagerly anticipating the opportunity to express the depth of my appreciation.To you, dear reader, a cascade of gratitude flows from the ink of every sentence. Your presence on this literary voyage infuses it with purpose and vitality. With each turn of the page, I am filled with anticipation, envisioning the moments we share as words transform into shared emotions, creating a tapestry of connection.

Table of contents

Introduction

In the fast-paced world of finance, where fortunes are made and lost in the blink of an eye, there are few individuals whose stories captivate our imagination and inspire us to dream big. David Tepper is one such individual—a man whose journey from humble beginnings to financial prominence is a testament to the power of perseverance, passion, and unwavering belief in oneself.

Imagine a world where opportunity beckons from every corner, where the promise of success hangs in the air like a tantalizing fragrance. It's a world where dreams are born, where fortunes are made, and where the bold and the fearless rise to the top. This is the world of David Tepper—a world of endless possibilities, where the only limit is the depth of one's ambition. But David Tepper's story is more than just a tale of financial success. It's a story of resilience in the face of adversity, of determination in the pursuit of one's dreams, and of the unwavering belief that anything is possible with hard work and perseverance. Born and raised in the steel city of Pittsburgh, Pennsylvania, David Tepper's upbringing was humble yet filled with love, support, and the belief that anything is possible with determination and hard work.

From a young age, Tepper demonstrated a natural curiosity and intellect, devouring books on economics and finance with an insatiable thirst for knowledge. As he grew older, Tepper's passion for finance only intensified, leading him to pursue a degree in economics from the University of Pittsburgh. But it was his move to Wall Street, the epicenter of the financial world, that would truly set him on the path to greatness. In the bustling streets of New York City, Tepper found himself surrounded by some of the brightest minds in finance, each vying for their place in the sun. But Tepper was different. He possessed a unique blend of intellect, intuition, and fearlessness that set him apart from the rest. And it wasn't long before he caught the attention of industry veterans, who recognized his potential and talent.

From his early days as a young investor to his rise as one of the most successful hedge fund managers of his generation, David Tepper's journey is a testament to the power of perseverance, passion, and unwavering belief in oneself. Through the highs and lows of the financial markets, Tepper remained steadfast in his pursuit of excellence, never allowing setbacks or obstacles to derail his dreams. But David Tepper's story is more than just a tale of financial success. It's a story of resilience in the face of adversity, of determination in the pursuit of one's dreams, and of the unwavering belief that anything is possible with hard work and perseverance.

As we embark on this journey into the life and career of David Tepper, let us be inspired by his example, encouraged by his resilience, and emboldened by his unwavering belief in the power of the human spirit. For in the world of finance and beyond, David Tepper's story reminds us that with passion, perseverance, and a little bit of luck, anything is possible.

Chapter One; Early Years: From Pittsburgh to Wall Street

David Tepper's journey from his humble beginnings in Pittsburgh to the bustling streets of Wall Street is a captivating tale of perseverance, ambition, and unwavering determination. Born on September 11, 1957, in the steel city of Pittsburgh, Pennsylvania, Tepper's upbringing was rooted in hard work and resilience.

Growing up in a modest household, Tepper learned the value of perseverance from a young age. His parents instilled in him the importance of education and the rewards of dedication and determination. Despite facing financial challenges, Tepper's family provided him with unwavering support, nurturing his dreams and aspirations.

From an early age, Tepper exhibited a keen intellect and a natural curiosity about the world of finance. While his peers were playing games, Tepper was devouring books on economics and investing, fascinated by the intricacies of the stock market and the potential for wealth creation.

After graduating from high school, Tepper's path to success took him to the esteemed halls of the University of Pittsburgh, where he pursued a degree in economics. It was during his time at university that Tepper's passion for finance truly flourished. He immersed himself in his studies, devouring every bit of knowledge he could find about the world of finance and investing. Upon graduating from university, Tepper set his sights on Wall Street, the epicenter of the financial world. With dreams of making it big in the world of finance, he packed his bags and headed to New York City, where he hoped to carve out a name for himself among the titans of Wall Street.

Tepper's early years on Wall Street were not without their challenges. Like many young professionals starting out in the competitive world of finance, he faced numerous setbacks and obstacles along the way. But true to his resilient nature, Tepper refused to be deterred by adversity.

Instead, he viewed each setback as an opportunity to learn and grow, honing his skills and refining his craft with each passing day. Through hard work, determination, and a relentless pursuit of excellence, Tepper began to make a name for himself on Wall Street. His keen intellect, sharp instincts, and fearless approach to investing caught the attention of industry veterans, who recognized his potential and talent. In 1993, Tepper took a bold leap of faith and founded his own hedge fund, Appaloosa Management L.P. Armed with nothing but his wits and a burning desire to succeed, Tepper set out to build a financial empire from the ground up. The early years of Appaloosa Management were not without their challenges. In the highly competitive world of hedge funds, success is never guaranteed, and failure lurks around every corner.

But Tepper's strategic brilliance and unwavering determination set him apart from the rest. He quickly established himself as a force to be reckoned with in the world of finance, earning a reputation for his uncanny ability to spot opportunities where others saw only risk. As his reputation grew, so too did his fortune. Tepper's strategic investments in distressed debt and undervalued assets yielded handsome returns, catapulting him to the upper echelons of the financial world. But despite his success, Tepper remained grounded and humble, never forgetting his roots or the values instilled in him by his family.

Today, David Tepper stands as a shining example of the American dream. From his humble beginnings in Pittsburgh to the pinnacle of success on Wall Street, his journey is a testament to the power of hard work, determination, and unwavering belief in oneself. And as he continues to chart new frontiers in the world of finance, one thing is certain: the story of David Tepper is far from over.

Chapter Two; Appaloosa Management L.P

A Hedge Fund Pioneer

Appaloosa Management L.P. stands as a testament to the vision, ingenuity, and strategic brilliance of its founder, David Tepper. Established in 1993, the hedge fund quickly rose to prominence in the financial world, earning a reputation for its bold investment strategies and impressive returns.

This article explores the journey of Appaloosa Management L.P., from its humble beginnings to its status as a pioneer in the world of hedge funds. The Genesis of Appaloosa Management L.P, The story of Appaloosa Management L.P, begins with David Tepper's unwavering belief in his ability to succeed in the world of finance. Armed with a wealth of knowledge, a keen intellect, and a fearless approach to investing, Tepper set out to establish his own hedge fund in the early 1990s. Driven by a desire to chart his own course and pursue his own investment strategies, Tepper founded Appaloosa Management L.P. in 1993. The name "Appaloosa" was inspired by the Native American horse breed known for its strength, agility, and endurance, qualities that Tepper sought to emulate in his approach to investing.

Early Challenges and Triumphs

In its early years, Appaloosa Management faced its fair share of challenges. Like any new venture, building a successful hedge fund from the ground up required perseverance, patience, and an unwavering commitment to excellence.

But despite the obstacles in his path, Tepper remained undeterred. Drawing on his vast knowledge of the financial markets and his keen instincts for spotting opportunities, he began to make a name for himself on Wall Street. One of the key factors behind Appaloosa Management's early success was Tepper's contrarian investment philosophy. While many investors shied away from risk, Tepper embraced it, recognizing that with risk comes opportunity. He was unafraid to take bold, calculated risks, often investing in distressed assets and undervalued securities that others overlooked.

Strategic Investments and Growth, As Appaloosa Management's reputation grew, so too did its assets under management. Tepper's strategic investments in distressed debt, bankruptcy restructurings, and corporate turnarounds yielded impressive returns for his investors, solidifying the hedge fund's position as a pioneer in the field.

One of the hallmarks of Appaloosa Management's investment strategy was its ability to identify undervalued assets and capitalize on market inefficiencies. Tepper and his team conducted rigorous research and analysis to uncover opportunities that others missed, giving them a competitive edge in the marketplace. But perhaps the most defining moment in Appaloosa Management's history came during the 2008 financial crisis. While many hedge funds faltered in the face of unprecedented market turmoil, Appaloosa Management thrived. Tepper's prescient investments in distressed financial institutions such as Bank of America and Citigroup earned the hedge fund billions of dollars in profits, cementing its reputation as a powerhouse in the industry.

Legacy and Impact

Today, Appaloosa Management L.P. stands as a shining example of what can be achieved through vision, determination, and strategic thinking. From its humble beginnings in 1993 to its status as a global leader in the world of hedge funds, the journey of Appaloosa Management is a testament to the entrepreneurial spirit and innovative mindset of its founder, David Tepper.

But beyond its financial success, Appaloosa Management's legacy lies in its commitment to excellence, integrity, and investor satisfaction. Throughout its history, the hedge fund has remained true to its founding principles, delivering consistent returns for its investors while upholding the highest standards of professionalism and ethical conduct.

As David Tepper continues to lead Appaloosa Management into the future, the hedge fund will remain at the forefront of the industry, pioneering new strategies, and setting new standards of excellence for generations to come.

Chapter Three; Mastering the Markets: Tepper's Bold Investments

David Tepper's mastery of the financial markets is a testament to his keen intellect, fearless approach to investing, and uncanny ability to spot opportunities where others see only risk. From his early years on Wall Street to his rise as a titan of finance, Tepper's bold investments have earned him a reputation as one of the most successful hedge fund managers of his generation. This article delves into Tepper's strategic brilliance and explores some of his most daring investments that have shaped his remarkable career.

The Early Years: A Foundation of Knowledge

Tepper's journey to mastering the markets began long before he founded his hedge fund, Appaloosa Management L.P. His insatiable curiosity and passion for finance led him to immerse himself in the intricacies of the financial markets from a young age.

During his time at the University of Pittsburgh, Tepper honed his analytical skills and deepened his understanding of economics and investing. He devoured books, dissected market trends, and absorbed every piece of information he could find about the world of finance. This early foundation of knowledge would prove invaluable as Tepper embarked on his career on Wall Street, armed with a deep understanding of the markets and a hunger for success.

Contrarian Investing: Embracing Risk, One of the hallmarks of Tepper's investment philosophy is his willingness to embrace risk and go against the grain. While many investors shy away from volatility and uncertainty, Tepper sees them as opportunities to capitalize on market inefficiencies.

Throughout his career, Tepper has made a name for himself by taking bold, contrarian positions that others deemed too risky. Whether investing in distressed debt, turnaround situations, or companies on the brink of bankruptcy, Tepper has consistently demonstrated a knack for spotting undervalued assets and turning them into profitable investments.

Navigating Turbulent Waters: The 2008 Financial Crisis

Perhaps the most defining moment in Tepper's career came during the 2008 financial crisis. While many hedge funds faltered in the face of unprecedented market turmoil, Tepper saw opportunity where others saw only despair.

Recognizing that the crisis had created significant dislocations in the market, Tepper made a series of bold investments that would cement his reputation as a savvy investor and earn his hedge fund billions of dollars in profits. One of Tepper's most notable investments during the crisis was his stake in struggling financial institutions such as Bank of America and Citigroup. While others were fleeing from these companies, Tepper saw potential for outsized returns and seized the opportunity with both hands.

His bet paid off handsomely, as both Bank of America and Citigroup rebounded strongly in the years following the crisis, delivering massive profits for Tepper and his investors.

Looking to the Future: Tepper's Vision for Success

As David Tepper continues to navigate the ever-changing landscape of the financial markets, his bold investments and fearless approach to investing remain as relevant as ever.

From his early days on Wall Street to his current position as one of the most influential figures in finance, Tepper's journey is a testament to the power of vision, determination, and strategic thinking. As he looks to the future, Tepper remains committed to pushing the boundaries of what is possible in the world of finance. Whether it's identifying emerging trends, uncovering hidden opportunities, or pioneering new investment strategies, one thing makes him Stand out.

David Tepper will continue to master the markets and leave an indelible mark on the world of finance for years to come.

Chapter Four; Beyond Finance: Exploring Tepper's Diverse Ventures

David Tepper's influence extends far beyond the realm of finance. While he is widely recognized as one of the most successful hedge fund managers of his generation, Tepper's interests and ventures span a diverse range of industries and pursuits. From his ownership of sports franchises to his philanthropic endeavors, this article delves into the multifaceted world of David Tepper beyond finance.

Owning Sports Franchises: The Carolina Panthers and Charlotte FC

One of David Tepper's most prominent ventures outside of finance is his ownership of sports franchises. In 2018, Tepper made headlines when he purchased the Carolina Panthers, a National Football League (NFL) team based in Charlotte, North Carolina.

Tepper's acquisition of the Panthers was met with widespread acclaim, as he brought a fresh perspective and a deep commitment to excellence to the franchise. Under his leadership, the Panthers have continued to thrive both on and off the field, fostering a culture of innovation, teamwork, and community engagement. In addition to the Panthers, Tepper also ventured into Major League Soccer (MLS) ownership with the founding of Charlotte FC. Announced in 2019, Charlotte FC became the newest expansion team in MLS, with Tepper at the helm as the principal owner.

Tepper's foray into sports ownership reflects his passion for athletics and his desire to make a positive impact in the communities where his teams are based. Through his ownership of the Panthers and Charlotte FC, Tepper has become a respected figure in the world of professional sports, using his platform to promote diversity, inclusion, and social responsibility.

Philanthropy: Tepper's Impact Beyond the Boardroom

Beyond his business ventures, David Tepper is also deeply committed to philanthropy and giving back to those in need. Throughout his career, Tepper has donated millions of dollars to charitable causes and organizations, with a particular focus on education, healthcare, and poverty alleviation.

Tepper's philanthropic efforts have touched countless lives, from funding scholarships for underprivileged students to supporting medical research and humanitarian aid initiatives. His generosity has made a tangible difference in communities around the world, demonstrating his belief in the power of giving back and making a positive impact on society. In addition to his personal philanthropy, Tepper has also established the David Tepper Charitable Foundation, which supports a wide range of causes and initiatives aimed at improving the lives of individuals and communities in need. Through his foundation, Tepper has helped to fund educational programs, healthcare services, and social welfare initiatives, leaving a lasting legacy of compassion and generosity.

A Legacy of Excellence and Impact, In conclusion, David Tepper's ventures beyond finance speak to his diverse interests, entrepreneurial spirit, and commitment to making a difference in the world. From his ownership of sports franchises to his philanthropic endeavors, Tepper's impact extends far beyond the boardroom, leaving a lasting legacy of excellence and impact in everything he touches. As he continues to explore new opportunities and pursue his passions,it is very likely that David Tepper will always be a force for positive change and innovation in the world.

Chapter Five; The Tepper Touch: Insights into His Investment Strategy

David Tepper's investment strategy is a reflection of his keen intellect, bold approach, and unwavering commitment to excellence. Over the years, Tepper has established himself as one of the most successful hedge fund managers in the world, earning a reputation for his ability to generate consistent returns in both bull and bear markets. This article offers insights into the key elements of Tepper's investment strategy and explores how he has navigated the complexities of the financial markets with his unique "Tepper Touch."

Embracing Opportunity Amidst Uncertainty

At the heart of David Tepper's investment strategy is his contrarian mindset. While many investors shy away from uncertainty and volatility, Tepper sees them as opportunities to capitalize on market inefficiencies and generate outsized returns.

Tepper is not afraid to go against the grain and take bold, contrarian positions that others may view as too risky. Whether it's investing in distressed debt, turnaround situations, or companies facing temporary setbacks, Tepper's willingness to embrace risk has been a key driver of his success. By betting against the consensus and identifying undervalued assets that others overlook, Tepper has been able to generate significant alpha for his investors, outperforming the broader market and delivering consistent returns over the long term.

Rigorous Research and Analysis: Uncovering Hidden Gems, Another hallmark of David Tepper's investment strategy is his commitment to rigorous research and analysis. Tepper and his team conduct exhaustive due diligence on potential investment opportunities, carefully analyzing financial statements, market trends, and industry dynamics to identify potential risks and opportunities.

Tepper's meticulous approach to research allows him to uncover hidden gems and identify undervalued assets that have the potential to deliver outsized returns. By digging deep into the fundamentals of companies and industries, Tepper is able to gain a comprehensive understanding of the factors driving their performance and make informed investment decisions accordingly.

Flexibility and Adaptability, In addition to his contrarian mindset and rigorous research, David Tepper's investment strategy is characterized by flexibility and adaptability. Tepper recognizes that the financial markets are dynamic and ever-changing, and he is not afraid to adjust his investment approach in response to shifting market conditions.

Whether it's pivoting to new investment opportunities, adjusting portfolio allocations, or hedging against potential risks, Tepper remains agile and nimble in his approach to investing. This flexibility allows him to capitalize on emerging trends and navigate changing market environments with ease, positioning his hedge fund for long-term success.

Focus on Risk Management: Preserving Capital in Turbulent Times

Despite his willingness to embrace risk, David Tepper is acutely aware of the importance of risk management in investing. Tepper employs a disciplined approach to risk management, using a combination of diversification, hedging, and position sizing to protect his investors' capital and preserve wealth in turbulent times.

Tepper's focus on risk management allows him to navigate market downturns and economic uncertainties with confidence, minimizing potential losses and preserving capital for future investment opportunities. By prioritizing downside protection and capital preservation, Tepper ensures that his hedge fund remains resilient and well-positioned to weather any storm.

The Art of Investing Tepper Style, In conclusion, David Tepper's investment strategy is a testament to his analytical prowess, contrarian thinking, and unwavering discipline. By embracing opportunity amidst uncertainty, conducting rigorous research and analysis, remaining flexible and adaptable, and prioritizing risk management, Tepper has established himself as a master of the financial markets.

Through his unique "Tepper Touch," he has consistently generated superior returns for his investors and cemented his reputation as one of the most successful hedge fund managers of his generation. As he continues to navigate the complexities of the financial markets, it is most definite that David Tepper's investment strategy will continue to be a source of inspiration and insight for investors around the world.

Chapter Six; Personal Insights: Understanding David Tepper

David Tepper, a prominent figure in the world of finance, is more than just a successful hedge fund manager. Behind the headlines and market moves lies a multifaceted individual whose personal insights and experiences have shaped his approach to business, investing, and life. This article offers a glimpse into the life and mind of David Tepper, providing valuable insights into what makes him tick and how he has become one of the most influential figures in finance today.

Early Influences: A Foundation of Resilience

David Tepper's journey to success began in Pittsburgh, Pennsylvania, where he was born on September 11, 1957. Growing up in a middle-class family, Tepper learned the value of hard work and resilience from a young age. His parents instilled in him a strong work ethic and a belief in the power of education and determination.

Despite facing financial challenges, Tepper's upbringing was filled with love, support, and encouragement. His parents encouraged him to pursue his passions and follow his dreams, laying the foundation for his future success in the world of finance. A Passion for Learning: The Road to Wall Street, From an early age, David Tepper demonstrated a natural curiosity and intellect. He was drawn to the world of finance and investing, devouring books and soaking up knowledge about the markets and economic trends.

After graduating from the University of Pittsburgh with a degree in economics, Tepper set his sights on Wall Street, the epicenter of the financial world. Determined to make a name for himself in the competitive world of finance, he packed his bags and headed to New York City, where he would begin his career as an investor.

The Tepper Touch: A Unique Approach to Investing

David Tepper's success as an investor can be attributed to his unique approach to investing, which combines rigorous analysis with bold, contrarian thinking. Unlike many investors who shy away from uncertainty and volatility, Tepper sees them as opportunities to capitalize on market inefficiencies and generate outsized returns.

Tepper's investment philosophy is grounded in a deep understanding of the fundamentals of companies and industries. He conducts thorough research and analysis to identify undervalued assets and potential opportunities that others may overlook. But perhaps the most defining aspect of Tepper's approach to investing is his willingness to take bold, contrarian positions. He is not afraid to go against the grain and bet against the consensus, often investing in distressed assets or turnaround situations that others deem too risky.

Beyond Finance: A Man of Many Interests, While David Tepper is best known for his success in the world of finance, he is also a man of many interests outside of the business world. He is an avid sports fan and owns the Carolina Panthers, a National Football League (NFL) team based in Charlotte, North Carolina.

Tepper's ownership of the Panthers reflects his passion for sports and his desire to make a positive impact in the communities where his teams are based. Under his leadership, the Panthers have thrived both on and off the field, fostering a culture of excellence, innovation, and community engagement. In addition to his sports ventures, David Tepper is also deeply committed to philanthropy and giving back to those in need. He has donated millions of dollars to charitable causes and organizations, with a particular focus on education, healthcare, and poverty alleviation.

In conclusion, David Tepper is much more than just a successful hedge fund manager. He is a man of many talents and interests, whose personal insights and experiences have shaped his approach to business, investing, and life. From his humble beginnings in Pittsburgh to his rise as a titan of finance, Tepper's journey is a testament to the power of hard work, determination, and resilience. And as he continues to make his mark on the world, one thing is Obvious, David Tepper's personal insights and unique approach to life will continue to inspire and influence others for generations to come.

Conclusion

In delving into the multifaceted world of David Tepper, we've uncovered not just the story of a successful hedge fund manager, but also the narrative of a resilient individual whose journey from humble beginnings to financial prominence is marked by determination, passion, and unwavering commitment.

Through exploring Tepper's early influences, investment strategies, personal insights, and diverse ventures, we've gained valuable insights into what drives him, how he navigates challenges, and the principles that guide his success. From his upbringing in Pittsburgh to his bold investments on Wall Street, Tepper's story is one of perseverance and tenacity. His ability to embrace risk, think outside the box, and seize opportunities where others see only obstacles has propelled him to the forefront of the financial world. But beyond his achievements in finance, Tepper's interests extend to sports ownership, philanthropy, and a commitment to making a positive impact on society.

Through his ownership of the Carolina Panthers and Charlotte FC, Tepper has left an indelible mark on the world of sports, fostering a culture of excellence, innovation, and community engagement. His philanthropic endeavors, driven by a desire to give back and make a difference, have touched countless lives and left a lasting legacy of compassion and generosity. As we conclude this journey into the life and mind of David Tepper, we are reminded of the power of perseverance, the importance of embracing risk, and the value of giving back. Tepper's story serves as an inspiration to all who dare to dream big and pursue their passions with unwavering determination.

To our readers, we extend our heartfelt gratitude for joining us on this odyssey through the life and career of David Tepper. We hope that you've found inspiration, insight, and perhaps even a new perspective on the world of finance and beyond.

Your support and engagement mean the world to us, and we welcome any feedback or reviews you may have on this book. If you've enjoyed this journey and found value in our exploration of David Tepper's story, we kindly ask for your support in the form of a positive review. Your feedback helps us continue to create compelling content and share inspiring stories with readers around the world.

Thank you once again for your time, your attention, and your interest in the remarkable life of David Tepper. May his story continue to inspire and empower you to pursue your own dreams and aspirations with courage, resilience, and unwavering belief in yourself.

Made in the USA
Las Vegas, NV
16 May 2024

89982528R00030